The Adventuresome Teenager's Guide to London

Susanna Evans
Richard Evans

Published by Bremerhaven Press

ISBN: 1979408440
ISBN 13: 9781979408448
Library of Congress Control Number: 2017960681
LCCN Imprint Name: Bremerhaven Press, Minneapolis

About the Authors

Susanna Evans is a high school junior in Milwaukee, Wisconsin. She's a rock climber and a sprinter on her varsity track team. In college she expects to minor in art and major in something that makes enough money to pay for more traveling. Her favorite food is anything Italian. Her weakness is spiders; she can't stand them.

Rich Evans is Susanna's dad. He lives in Minnesota with Susanna's little brother and sister. He's a rock climber too but certainly no sprinter. He majored in math at Syracuse University. His favorite food is anything low carb (how boring!). His weakness is—well, he doesn't have one. As a dad, he gets stuck with shooing spiders and the rest of the dirty work.

For Chaney and Jack

Contents

Left: The London Eye over the river Thames before the Silver Surfer trashed it in *The Fantastic Four: Rise of the Silver Surfer.*

Middle column: Not the typical view of a Trafalgar Square lion; a Trafalgar Square street artist; van Gogh's *Sunflowers* at the National Gallery.

Right column: A tunnel on the Tube; cars and a boat passing under the clear floor of the Tower Bridge; Dior—need I say more?

Top row: Big Ben, but raise your camera if you want an actual shot with Big Ben; in Greenwich, I'm on the Eastern Hemisphere, and my cousin is on the Western Hemisphere; jet-lagged on the Underground.

Middle row: Platform 9¾ at King's Cross Station; these classic London phone boxes are dirty, look around for a clean one; thank God that M&Ms are everywhere in the world.

Bottom row: Disney is everywhere too; on the Underground— you'll figure this out soon enough; it's hard to look good in O'Hare airport.

Top row: A horse guardsman—it's OK to pet the horse but not the guardsman; high tea at Brown's Hotel; Big Ben at sunset.

Middle row: Thoughtful at the National Gallery; London pizza is European in style—this one wasn't sliced for us; always ride on the top.

Bottom row: A Covent Garden performer; Italian architecture at Covent Garden; don't be crass and spit your gum on London, which is a very clean city.

Touring London Parent-Free

For some reason, parents get more worried about family safety the farther from home the family gets. Parents would hold your hand in Mr. Rogers's neighborhood if it took a plane ride to get there.

London is not on the moon, but tell that to parents. They make a big deal about the trip. It's cool, sure, but the flight from Boston to London is six and a half hours—an hour shorter than driving from Boston to Washington, DC.

London is just New York City or Los Angeles but with better public transportation and safer streets. London has the same population as NYC—about eight million. Just think, you could be flying fourteen hours to Tokyo, a place crammed with thirty-nine million people, all of them thinking they're late to work all the time. London's not too much like that, even during rush hour.

That weird parent-brain safety malfunction makes getting some time and space for yourself in London a problem. I was lucky for a change. My dad has been to London enough times to be comfortable there and to not worry too much about me exploring the place alone. He sent me off with only one warning: "Don't go off with anybody you don't know, especially in a car."

That's pretty funny, since he knew I didn't know anyone in London. I figured you, the reader of this book, wouldn't have it so easy to get a little space for yourself away from your parents. So here I am passing along some stuff I learned about London to convince your parents to give you some independence there, even if that means just leaving them a little early to get back to the hotel to message friends back home.

Also, I like to do different things than my parents do. I can get through museums, churches, and galleries a lot faster than them. When I've seen all I want to see, I don't want to hang around the museum and wait for them. If you've seen one old Bible, you've seen them all. I like to take off, to chill, to eat gelato, and to watch street performers in Trafalgar Square.[1]

Taking off is easy to do in London. Almost everyone speaks English with an understandable accent,[2] and all the signs are in English. British money works like dollars and cents, but it's called pounds and pence. Police are everywhere tourists go; violent crime in those areas is practically zero. If you want trouble, you'll have to make it yourself.

So your parents don't have to be scared to let you go off on your own. All you have to do is show them that you will be safe. Let them know that you know how to take care of yourself in London. Knowledge is power; this book gives you that power.

---

[1] It's a big public square named after the great 1805 British naval victory over a French and Spanish fleet in the waters off southern Spain. The British admiral was Lord Nelson, and the square is marked with Nelson's Column. I could never figure out why they built a column so tall that Nelson, at the top, is hard to see. The lions at the base were added later.

[2] Except for some of the Scots and Irish, but you probably won't run into any of them.

Before Traveling to London

Don't even bother trying to tell your parents that London is no big deal (unless you want to get them mad). Do a little reverse psychology. Show your parents that you understand that London is different from home. There are a few things you need to do and some things to get organized before you go. It's not a lot, and it's fun.

Get a Phone Charger Adapter

The prongs on your phone charger are different than British ones, so you'll need a simple adapter (packs of three are ten bucks on Amazon) to put on the prongs of your charger to convert it to fit British wall sockets.[3] It might seem crazy for your family to buy several adapters for what is probably your only trip to London, but life is a whole lot easier if everyone has his or her own adapter. It's a cheap way to keep the peace.

Get a Debit Card

London is no different than home. Breaking out costs money: money for the Underground, money for lunch and chocolate, money to donate to national museums,[4] and money to buy stuff. So you have to have money. Nearly every store and restaurant in London takes debit and credit cards, so get one (or both) before the trip. Your parents can probably get you your own bank account linked to theirs that comes with a debit card. But there is always cash. Exchange US dollars for pounds at the British airport you land in, or better yet, use

---

[3] British wall sockets often have switches, like light switches. You'll need to plug in and turn the switch on.

[4] A lot of these are free but have donation boxes near their entrances. British coins are annoyingly heavy, and donating them to the museum is a good way to get rid of them.

the ATM in the airport to get a few pounds on your way into London.

Britain's "dollar" is called a pound. Its symbol is £. The pound is made up from pence, which are like cents, and one hundred of them make a pound. Locals say "pee" instead of pence, as in "The gum costs fifty pee." The pence symbol is a "p," as in 50p for fifty pence. A pound is called a "quid," a five-pound note is called a "fiver," and a ten-pound note is called a "tenner."

The safest way to carry money in London is with a debit card (or a credit card if your parents will give you one). If it gets stolen, your parents can cancel it without losing any money. Nearly every store takes debit cards, as do the Underground ticket kiosks where you can recharge or buy a ticket. Street artists don't take debit cards. You'll have to pay them cash. I'd say carry twenty pounds cash or so in your front pocket and a debit card.

Twenty pounds[5] (£20) is about $26.[6] That means a pretty £100 dress in a shop window really costs $130. Unlike at home, tax is almost always included, so a £20 item is really £20, unless a tag or sign says "EX VAT," which means "excluding the value-added tax." If the sign says "EX VAT," the thing will cost the price plus some more for the tax, just like here in America. But most of the stuff you buy will cost what it says it costs.

---

[5] Sometimes prices are in "pounds sterling." That's the same as pounds.

[6] The pounds to dollars exchange rates change. Before you leave the United States, Google "What is ten pounds in USD?" to get the conversion of ten pounds to US dollars. As this book is written, £10 = $12.95. Round it up to $13. Now you can easily estimate a rough check of prices. A £50 shirt is five times $13 = $65. For lower-priced items, move the decimal point. If £10 is $13, then £1 is $1.30. So a £2 chocolate bar is two times $1.30 = $2.60.

Get the Right Paperwork

You'll need a current passport, of course, but if your family name is different from the adults you are traveling with (e.g., your boyfriend's family or an uncle with a different last name), the British authorities will need some evidence that you weren't abducted by your adult traveling companion.

According to the UK government website,[7] you can prove this with:

- A birth or adoption certificate showing your relationship to the guardian
- If the guardian is your parent, the guardian can bring his or her divorce or marriage certificates showing the name change.
- A letter, with contact details, from your parents giving permission for you to travel to Britain with the guardian

My cousin, who has a different family name than mine, traveled with us to London. Our British passport control officer not only wanted to see a letter from her mom but also wanted her mom's signature in my cousin's passport to compare the signatures on the letter and on the passport. We forgot the letter and got into the country only because we looked honest (I guess) and incredibly naive and because we showed our return tickets home to Chicago. But we held up the people behind us in line for a long time.

Set Up Your Smartphone

Your smartphone is your camera and your Internet access. It's also a way to call emergency services. In Europe and the

---

[7] https://www.gov.uk/uk-border-control/before-you-leave-for-the-uk, as of September 2017

United Kingdom, calling 112 from any mobile phone should get you help. It's just like 911 in the United States. If it's not an emergency, but you need help, call 101. Those numbers should work dialed just like that from your cell phone, and you might want to put them in your contacts and make them favorites so you don't have to remember them in an emergency.

Clear some memory to make room for photos, and install some apps: WhatsApp for messaging home and Skype for calling home. If you already have Snapchat, use it for messaging and Internet calling.

Make a Playlist and Watch Some Movies

Get psyched about London by making a London-song playlist and by watching some movies about London before you travel. Watching movies set in London is great because places you've seen on the screen will take on a familiar feel once you are there in real life. Personally, guidebooks are boring, and I'd rather watch *Notting Hill* or *Captain America* to see a place than to read about it in Rick Steves's travel book on London. And yet here I am writing a travel book, expecting you to read it.

Make a Playlist

If you aren't sure where to begin, Google "songs about London." There are a million of them in every genre. Below are five old ones your parents might like. Get your friends to help you find some newer songs, but it's going to take a lot more than five songs to listen to on the long flight to London, which is 140 songs long from NYC to London.

Find songs with London in the name, songs about London, songs by British bands, or songs recorded live in London. For

extra points, listen to some songs recorded live at the Royal
Albert Hall and then visit the Hall.

1. "Werewolves of London" by Warren Zevon. You have to
   love Zevon's howl. Trader Vic's is a tropical-themed
   bar in the Mayfair part of London, just north of
   Wellington Arch. It's been around for decades; check it
   out. Trader Vic's is known for mai tais, but Zevon
   mentions piña coladas in his song. Both are rum
   drinks.

2. "West End Girls" by Pet Shop Boys. I put this song in
   because I thought it was about the theater district—
   the West End. Nope. It's a social justice song, I think,
   with lots of arcane references. Anyway, it's British
   enough to have been performed at the closing
   ceremonies of the 2012 London Summer Olympics.

3. "Play With Fire" by the Rolling Stones. This song, by a
   British band, mentions St. John's Wood, which isn't a
   forest but a wealthy neighborhood in Westminster.
   You'll be in Westminster, so go check out St. John's
   Wood. Maybe you'll see a Rolls-Royce drive by. St.
   John's Wood residents pay the highest average rent in
   London.

4. "London Calling" by the Clash. This is punk at its best,
   but you should also listen to "Rock the Casbah,"
   which is a better song.[8] *London Calling* is also the
   name of the album. The album was ranked at number
   eight on *Rolling Stone*'s list "The 500 Greatest Albums
   of All Time." *London Calling* was a top ten album in the
   United Kingdom. The funny thing is that when the

---

[8] A casbah (or kasbah) is a walled citadel found in North African
cities. The most famous one is in Algiers, Algeria. So now you have
the first song in your playlist for a trip to Algeria.

Clash recorded the album, they didn't act very punk-like. They were disciplined and organized.

5. "London Belongs to Me" by Saint Etienne. There is a film with the same name from 1948 and a fan YouTube slideshow video with lots of great pictures of London. Saint Etienne is an indie dance band from the early 1990s, but "London Belongs to Me" isn't a dance song, at least not for me. It depends on how you dance. But it's a pretty song.

Watch Some Movies

London is the centerpiece of a whole lot of movies. There will absolutely be some films you'll like—and some you won't. *A Clockwork Orange*, for example, is famous but way too weird to watch. Google "movies with London in them," and you'll get websites suggesting dozens of London films. Some are old, and I watch newer ones because places look the same, except with they are digitally blown up in explosions. And newer movies are better than old ones. Just sayin'.

If you like romance movies, Google "romance movies filmed in London," and two are sure to pop up: *Notting Hill* and *Bridget Jones's Diary*. Funnily enough, Hugh Grant is in both of those movies. Neither movies show the famous, touristy parts of London—the parts you're bound to see. However, if you really like those movies, you can find tour companies that will take you around London to off-the-beaten-path movie locations. Below is a very short list of movies I liked. They are action films.

1. *Skyfall*, a James Bond movie, has great views of the Thames and the MI6 building. Stand on the Vauxhall Bridge for the exact view of MI6 from the movie. It's a real spy building, so it doesn't have a big sign saying

what it is. I don't think it has any sign. Also, the National Gallery is in the movie.

2. *London Has Fallen* has famous buildings from all over London getting blown up. Plus, you'll get to see the bird's-eye view of them, which is not really possible on your trip.

3. *Thor: The Dark World* totally destroys Greenwich at the end of the movie. This is the movie to watch if you're going to visit Greenwich. If you like boats, go to Greenwich.

4. *V for Vendetta.* Goodbye, Parliament buildings.

5. *Captain America* shows Trafalgar Square. It's the square as it is now, but the setting is 1945, if that makes sense. You'll see.

6. *Fantastic Four: Rise of the Silver Surfer* has great views of the London Eye—falling down. It might be better to watch this one after you've taken the ride.

Traveling to London

Airport Security

In the United States, airport security is usually the same for international and domestic flights. If you've flown before, security should be about the same. People are always rushed and sometimes cranky going through airport security, so I look ahead in the line and see what I need to do to get through. Right after a TSA officer checks your ID and boarding pass, there will be a stack of gray bins to put your stuff in. That's when I start loosening my shoes and taking them off. I always wear socks so I don't have to stand barefoot, catching all the germs and fungus where other sockless people stood barefooted waiting to get their bodies' scanned.

Another guard will probably be shouting instructions: "Take off your shoes, belts, and jacket, and take everything out of your pockets and put them in a bin. Put larger electronics, like laptops, in a gray bin. No liquids larger than three ounces[9] and all liquids must fit in a quart-sized bag."

The guard will repeat that over and over again, but people still mess up all the time, especially accidently leaving on their belts and forgetting stuff in their pockets. Also, take off any jewelry and anything metal in your hair.

All your stuff goes through an x-ray machine on a conveyor belt. You'll walk in sock feet through a body scanner and then wait a second for the results. The scanner is sensitive

---

[9] Bring a travel bottle of hand sanitizer to carry on the plane, less than three ounces in size, just for the trip over and back. Airports are nasty. I spent a night in the Las Vegas airport while three people around me barfed.

and flags zippers, buckles, and even a little extra sweat. My dad is sweaty, and he's always getting busted for it.

If the machine flags problem areas on your body, the guard at the scanner exit will want to touch some parts of your body, so don't wear lots of layers, bulky sweaters, pants with lots of pockets, or underwire bras. If you wear bulky clothes, the TSA officer is just going to dig a little deeper or make you take off the clothing.

When you are cleared from the scanner, take your stuff out of the bins (you can leave the bins on the conveyor belt), and walk a little ways to some benches to recombobulate. Now you are done with security until the flight home. Even if you layover in Dublin or another city, as long as you don't leave security in that airport, you are finished with security.

Waiting for Departure

You'll probably have to wait a couple of hours in the airport before your flight leaves. Find your gate, leave your bag with your parents at the gate, and then try and find a charging station for your electronics. Your plane may or may not have a working power outlet[10] near your seat. The airport may be your last charge for six or more hours.

Sometimes airports have great charging areas, and sometimes you have to go looking under chairs and tables and in hallways to find outlets. It can be kind of fun and something to do. Some airports have tables with seats next to

[10] Bring your London plug adapter in your carryon luggage. Most of the time, the shape of the outlet on the plane matches the country the plane comes from. For example, United Airlines will have US-style outlets, and British Airways has the two-pin, UK-style plug. Even if you are not near an outlet on the plane, or if your plane doesn't have outlets, or if your adapter doesn't fit, you'll want your adapter with you in London just in case your luggage gets lost.

outlets. If someone is in the seat but next to an open outlet, it's OK to politely ask to use the outlet. Plug in, leave your phone there, move back, and watch it charge from a distance. Watching your phone charge should be the least exciting part of the trip.

Don't worry about someone stealing your phone. Everyone in an airport is either a passenger (who has paid a lot for a plane ticket) or an employee. I'm sure that crimes of convenience happen, but with all of the security and cameras, it would be foolish for a dedicated criminal to pay for a plane ticket and then to go to an airport looking to steal. I wouldn't walk away from my phone, but no one is going to snatch your phone and run.

When your phone is charged, go to the bathroom[11] (Do I really need to tell you that?), and then do some window shopping at the airport stores. They are outrageously expensive, but it's fun to look around. Some stores will have tourist stuff, while others may have high-end clothes and electronics. It depends on how big your airport is.

Bring snacks from home. Airport food is expensive (I've seen $1.25 for a banana; that's a 500 percent markup over the grocery store price) and not always healthy. Don't forget that some food, like liquids, isn't allowed through security. I've seen overripe bananas rejected by security and tossed in the trash. You might want your own food on the plane as well just in case you don't like the plane food. The plane will be short on chocolate too.

---

[11] You will have to stay seated on the plane for at least an hour from boarding until the plane reaches cruising altitude and the Captain turns off the seatbelt sign. That means there will be no way to use the plane's bathroom for a while.

On the Plane

There will probably be an outlet to charge your phone on the base of the seat in front of you, or maybe under your seat, but it might require the UK adapter, so be sure to bring it on the plane in your carryon bags.

Flight attendants will serve food on the plane (probably dinner and breakfast if you leave from the East Coast), but you might want more food or different food or candy. The food will start coming out (dinner if you are flying overnight, and most flights to London are overnight) probably an hour or so into the flight. After that, settle back, take your shoes off,[12] and watch a movie. Newer planes will have personal TV screens in the seatback in front of you,[13] and older planes will have TV monitors overhead.

At some point during the movie you may want to use the plane's bathroom.[14] Some people like to brush their teeth in there and change into pajamas. I pass on the pajamas and the teeth. That's your call; do whatever works for you.

If the movies suck, or if you just want to sleep, slowly recline your seat and try to sleep. My problem with sleeping on a plane is that as soon as I doze off my head flops over and I wake up. Some people like horseshoe-shaped pillows, but they don't fit snugly enough to keep my head from flopping.

---

[12] Only do this if your feet don't stink. Mine don't, but my dad brings a fresh pair of socks to change into on the plane so he can take off his shoes. Some people change into those treaded socks.
[13] If you have that, you can pick your own movie. Otherwise, you watch what everyone else watches. Bring your own earbuds or headphones. The airline should give you a junky pair of earbuds, but those break pretty fast.
[14] They can get disgusting by the end of the flight.

On some planes the headrest folds up on each side to grip my head, and that works OK but not great because then I can't shift my body because my head is locked up. Basically, don't count on a lot of sleep unless the plane is empty enough to stretch out across several seats.

That's often easy to do if you watch for a spot. Once the plane's doors close on the ground, you can get up and change your seat without asking the flight crew. Just do it.[15] If someone shows up, you can always move back to your reserved seat. You won't lose that seat.

Once you are in your seat, and as the plane is still loading, keep looking for seats with space around them, and then jump into them as soon as it looks like no more passengers are boarding. If you don't jump into those seats, someone else will. My dad is five feet ten and can sleep OK across three seats, but he has no flexibility at all and practically creaks when he wakes up. Just remember that you will probably fart in your sleep. Also, make sure someone wakes you for breakfast, which is often served just before landing. If you don't wake up, the flight attendants might pass you by.

Passport Control and Customs

After you land, you'll get off the plane and go through passport control.[16] That's where the authorities check your passport to make sure you are legally allowed to enter the country. They may ask a few questions—"How long are you staying? Where are you staying?"—but usually it's no big deal unless your family's paperwork is out of order. If it is, that's

---

[15] As the plane loads, warn your parents that you are going to attempt to find more room.

[16] Phone use isn't allowed in passport control or customs, including taking pictures.

really your parent's or guardian's problem. If that happens, stand back, and keep your mouth shut. Be invisible.

If they let you in the country, the next stop is customs. Customs should be no big deal; just don't bring in rough diamonds, meat, dairy products, or the obvious stuff like drugs and guns. We bypass customs because we have nothing to declare. We are travelers bringing our own stuff into England. Once through customs, you are officially in Britain with lots of adrenaline and excitement—and with severe jet lag.

Jet Lag

There is a five-hour time difference between New York and London, so it may be even more for you. It's a six-hour difference for me in Chicago. If your plane lands in London at 9:00 a.m., it feels like 5:00 a.m. to Easterners, 4:00 a.m. to Midwesterners, and 2:00 a.m. to Californians because that's the time back home and the time your body thinks it is. You didn't sleep well on the plane, so by noon London time you've been up for at least twenty-four hours. That means you'll be super sleepy and will want to go to bed. Don't do it. There are many ideas on how to minimize jet lag, but I don't think any work very well, except to try to train your body to London time and to keep London hours.

The really bad part is that you'll fall fast asleep at about 8:00 p.m. because you are super tired. But to your body that's just a nap at about 2:00 p.m. home time. So at 1:00 p.m. or so, you'll wake up refreshed from your "nap" because it's only late afternoon at home, which is way too early for your body to be in bed.

When I wake up in the middle of the night in London, I watch Netflix until I fall asleep at about 4:00 a.m. London time.

Then I get up at 8:00 a.m.[17] for a shower and breakfast. Absolutely do not sleep in, even though your body thinks it's around 2:00 a.m. By the way, the hotel toilet will probably flush with buttons—one for less water and one for more water. No explanation needed.

The experts say that it takes about five days in London for someone from the East Coast to fully recover from jet lag. You'll have to do it much faster than that.

---

[17] Get-up time depends on what you are doing for the day. Some things open early; some don't.

Touring London

What You'll Remember about London

It seems ironic that a guidebook author is suggesting that you don't follow the guidebook and just be spontaneous, but that's what I'm telling you. The things that I remember most about London weren't planned: getting lost in the West End on the way to St. Martin's Theater and nearly missing *The Mousetrap*, as well as ditching my dad on the Underground after high tea to go to the London Eye. Don't worry; he made it home OK.

If you can, use this book as an outline of what to do, not a map of what to do. For at least a couple of days on your trip, try and not be sure exactly how to get somewhere. Set yourself up for adventures—those are the things that you'll really remember. Polar explorer Roald Amundsen gave the fun formula. He is reported to have said, "Adventure is just bad planning." So don't plan too well.

Maps

Carry two maps—an Underground map and a map of London marked with the major landmarks and Underground station locations. If you plan on ditching your parents, be sure to bring your own maps. You can print an Underground map off the Internet, which works OK, but a home-printed map of London will be too small to read. I bought mine on Amazon.

Electronics

You only need one electronic device in London: your phone. Just like at home, it's your camera, downtime entertainment, and connection to friends. London is wet, so bring a baggie to cover your phone in the rain. If you use your phone a lot, make sure you've cleared out some memory, and bring an external battery (which works great on the plane too). Charging your phone at the hotel is easy—just plug your usual phone charger into an adapter,[18] and plug the adapter into the wall. You don't need to worry about volts and things like that. Sometimes UK outlets have on-and-off switches, so turn the switch on.

US phone companies charge expensive international roaming charges for background data usage on wireless and voice calls too, so the best advice is to run your phone in airplane mode with Wi-Fi turned back on. That way your smartphone is still your camera and can still communicate when you are at a hotspot.[19]

Communicating with Home

Don't forget that there's at least a six-hour time difference between London and your home in the United States. You are really going to irritate someone back home by messaging them at 10:00 a.m. London time.

In London, you can use Wi-Fi or wireless to message friends. Wi-Fi has the same benefit and problem in London as it does at home: it's free, but it's never around when you need it, like on a street or in a car.

Wi-Fi

Your hotel will have Wi-Fi, but it might not be free. If it's not free, have your parents buy the Wi-Fi so you all can watch

---

[18] A UK adapter has either two or three round pins in a row on one end and slots for your plug on the other end.
[19] Google "public hotspots in London" to get an idea of what's available.

Netflix or YouTube late at night as you work off jet lag and get acclimated to London time and upload your day's photos. Late evening in London is afternoon back home, so that's a good time to chat with friends.

Have your friends install Skype and whatever message app you use, like Snapchat or WhatsApp,[20] and message them from your hotel or public hotspot. Some message apps will work offline, so you can send messages all day long in London, and they will save up and go out when you connect back to Wi-Fi. WhatsApp does that, but Snapchat doesn't do it reliably.

Wireless

Sending and receiving data while roaming on your phone's wireless[21] is extremely expensive but very tempting to do because it means freedom from Wi-Fi hotspots. While roaming, you could use your phone just like you do at home. So if you can afford it, roam with your wireless plan in London. You might need to add 011 to the beginning of US phone numbers to connect to the United States.

There are some alternatives. US wireless carriers offer short-term international data plans, but these are still expensive. Once in London, you can rent a UK phone or buy a UK SIM card that fits your unlocked phone. Google "international data plans" for more wireless ideas.

I do the cheap and easy thing and turn my wireless off but keep my Wi-Fi on. On some kinds of phones, it's possible to restrict background data to save on roaming charges.

---

[20] Sometimes message apps, like iMessage, don't work across platforms on Wi-Fi, so it's best to get one that does so ahead of time, like WhatsApp.
[21] Some phone models and wireless carriers don't work with UK wireless technology, so you'll be limited to Wi-Fi.

Communicating with Your Parents

No, I don't mean this in some psychological sense; I mean actually calling your parents. This is the big stumbling block to touring some of London without your parents. After a day or so of traveling with them, if they could call you whenever they wanted to, they would probably let you go off by yourself.

In London, cell phones act like they are in the United States, so call your parents' cell phones as you would back home.[22] You don't need any extra numbers, such as country codes. The same goes for calling or texting friends at home in the United States.

I suggest turning on the wireless for your phones but not using it unless there is an emergency. Before the trip, for your phone and your parents' phones, see if you can figure out how to limit background data use but still have it work as a phone. Then, as you split to go do your thing in London, set the phones up so that you can call each other but not spend a ton of money on background data.

Texting in London, both to home and to your parents, should be cheap or free, depending on your wireless carrier back home. Just plan to text your parents where you are whenever you change locations. That's a cheap and easy solution. But use the SMS version of texting, not some other way, like Snapchat, unless your parents know how to use Snapchat.

Communicating to London Phones and Emergency Services

---

[22] It's a good idea to try this before going on an adventure.

Your smartphone is not only your camera and your Internet access, but it's also a way to call emergency services. In Europe and the United Kingdom, calling 112 from any mobile phone should get you help. It's just like 911 in the United States.

If the problem is not an emergency but you need help, call 101. Those numbers should work dialed just like that from your cell phone, but you might want to put them in your contacts and make them favorites so you don't have to remember them in an emergency.

To call your hotel or restaurant or another London number, you might need to add the "+44" country number in front of the local number.

How to call is easy to remember if you think of your cell phone as being in a little American bubble floating in London. Calling a US number doesn't change. But you'd better try all that before you really need it. Cell phones and service carriers can all be a little different.

What to Wear

Let's say you've eaten breakfast at the hotel,[23] and it's time to leave the hotel. London rains a lot, and I like umbrellas more than raincoats (unless it's chilly) because you can shake water off an umbrella[24] and fold it up whenever you enter a museum or whatever. A wet raincoat is a little harder to carry in a museum. A raincoat drips on other people when you bump against them.

---

[23] If you don't eat breakfast in your hotel, see my suggestions for breakfast in the "food" section of this book.
[24] I pack one of those little collapsible umbrellas, but you can buy umbrellas all over London if you forgot one. Your hotel might even lend you one.

You'll be walking a lot, so wear clothes and shoes that are comfortable for wet walking. Beyond that, London is filled with travelers and tourists from every country in the world, so fashion isn't an issue. You won't look weird, and no one cares what you wear. Everyone wears his or her own fashion from his or her own country, and England itself doesn't really have any wardrobe rules.[25]

The one exception might be dressing up a bit for high tea, perhaps in a simple cocktail dress and flats or a tie and nonjean pants with shoes. Also, I personally would not go to my hotel's breakfast in my pajamas, slippers, and robe, but I've seen it done.

Getting Lost

I could say that getting lost in London is a good thing. But it's not when you're running late for high tea at Brown's Hotel because, don't forget, you don't have your phone's GPS (no wireless) for help.

You'll see that street signs are on building corners, not necessarily on the street itself. Now that you know that, just look at your map and go, using big landmarks, like Big Ben, the London Eye, and the river Thames, to give you clues to your progress along the streets. Landmarks are pretty much what London is about and should be on your map. Use them as lighthouses. Sometimes I get from one place to another by leapfrogging past the landmarks that are between them. That way, if I get lost, I'm not seriously lost.

---

[25] This is unlike South America, where men don't usually wear shorts or jeans, or Papua New Guinea, where women wear short sleeves but keep their shoulders covered.

If you get seriously lost, have someone point to where you are on your map or ask directions to the nearest Underground station, go there, figure out where you are, and start over. But that will make you very late for high tea.

Traveling Alone: Transportation

The Underground

In any city, the people on a subway car are a selfie of that city's people. Sure, the very rich aren't riding the Underground, like us gophers, but everyone else does. When you ride London's Underground, you'll see every possible skin color and hear languages that you don't recognize. It's thrilling in its own way to have the world crushed down so small as to fit on a subway car.

Check out the other riders' demeanors too. Riders on the Washington, DC Metro[26] act like they think they don't deserve to be there and can't wait to get off. I don't get that feeling on the Underground. Riders on the Underground seem a bit more tolerant of it, like they are riding because they want to, not because they have to. But they probably have to ride just the same as the Americans have to ride the Metro. I've seen a lot more vermin on the Metro tracks than on the Underground tracks. Coincidence? Maybe.

In the Metro or the Underground, I've never seen vermin (human or animal) inside the cars—they are safe. Both systems' cars have the same level of grubbiness inside, which I think is a tolerable amount. But if I dropped a grape on the floor, I'd let it roll away. There is no five-second rule on the

---

[26] The Underground was up and running one hundred years before the Metro. My great-grandmother hid in the Underground for safety during the London Blitz in 1940, when the Germans bombed London every night for eight months.

Underground—it's too gross. You're not supposed to eat on the Underground anyway.

In both cities, people hurry on and off the trains. It's harder getting off the train and out of the station than getting on the right one. Getting off at the right stop is easy, but when you step off the train, there will be more than one exit, and people will be streaming toward the exits, carrying you with them. Floating with them out the wrong exit will land you on the wrong side of the street from where you want to be or on the opposite end of a city block from where you want to be. That's no big deal, but it is annoying, especially in the rain.

If it's your first day in London, hang out with your parents, but make sure you ride the Underground with them. That's key because the Underground is independence. Here are the three steps to use to get your parents to let you travel on the Underground by yourself.

Step one. Before leaving home in America, mention a few times how easy and safe the Underground is. If they ask how you know, mention this book. That will soften them up to the idea of you riding the Underground alone.

Step two. In London, travel on the Underground a few times with your parents. The first time, let them lead the way, but after that read the map, figure out where you are, lead the way onto the right train, and exit at the correct station. Be the Underground maven. That way your parents actually see that you can find your way around using the Underground. They will be impressed. You'll need an Underground map and a map of London, and both are easy to print out before you leave home or in an Underground station.

Step three. Now that your parents see that you know your way around the Underground, wait until it's time to go back to the hotel, and ask to leave ten minutes before them to meet them at the hotel. Show them on the Underground map that you know the right stops and that you know how to get from the destination station to the hotel. I act a little dismissive doing that kind of thing for effect, but you know your parents better than I do. Do what you need to.

Meet them back at the hotel. This is not the time to play a joke and disappear. Now you've shown your parents that you can travel by yourself. If they are still a little hesitant to let you go other places, show them on maps that you know how to get to and from stations to the places you want to go.

Like I said earlier, one thing that isn't on the maps is how to exit the destination station. Underground stations have several exits. Once you are at your destination station and get off the train, the next tricky part is figuring out which exit to use. Hopefully there will be a sign pointing out the exit to the place you are going, like to the British Museum. Sometimes you just have to exit, look at a London map, and figure out where to go or ask someone. But don't ask someone in a hurry. Ask another American or a Dutch person. They are nice, and they speak English well.

The London Underground map has colored lines representing train routes,[27] but each line has trains going in both directions. The only tricky part is getting on the one going in the right direction. If you get on the wrong one, you'll probably realize it right away, so get off at the next stop, walk across the platform, and get on the train going in the right direction. It doesn't cost more money to do that. The

[27] The routes are also named. For example, the dark blue-colored line is the Victoria line. The automatic voice on the train will say the route name and destination, not the color of the line. Sometimes a location name is spelled much differently than it's pronounced.

Underground gate scans your card—called an Oyster card—when you go below ground and when you come up again. You'll pay for an Oyster card from a machine in a kiosk in any station at the beginning of your stay in London.

You can tell the correct train direction because the side of the train has a lighted sign that is the last stop on the line. That tells you where it is going, and you want your destination in that direction. For example, if you are taking the Victoria line (dark blue) from Green Park to Leicester Square,[28] take the train headed to Cockfosters. Or ask someone if a particular train is going where you want to go.

And remember, "Mind the gap." You'll figure that out when you ride the Underground.

Buses and River Buses.

Your Oyster card will pay for buses and for transportation on the Thames River on river buses, which are large passenger boats that operate from twenty-one piers along the river. If you are traveling to a place near the river, a river bus is the way to go. The wait can be a bit longer than for an Underground train, but the view is great, and it's fun to ride the boats, which are so big that there is no chance of getting seasick. If traveling to Greenwich or the Globe Theater, consider riding on a river bus.

Uber

If the worst case scenario happens, and you are confused about getting somewhere, take a taxi[29] or an Uber[30] if your

---

[28] It is pronounced "lester" square.

[29] London taxi drivers (not Ubers) have to take an extremely hard knowledge test about the London streets and landmarks, known as "the test."

[30] By the time you read this book, London might have banned Uber

app works in London. It should, but try and use it on Wi-Fi to save on expensive international roaming charges.

Safety

London is very safe—except for American jaywalkers.[31] London drivers are really good about stopping for pedestrians in crosswalks, but if you decide to jaywalk, look out. Cars drive on the left side of the road, and it's really weird and unexpected to have cars coming at you from the right side after spending your whole life looking left just before stepping into the street.

If you've made it across a street OK, then you are just one of millions of tourists wandering around the city, and everyone will ignore you, except possibly thieves and people selling selfie sticks or flowers. I just say, "No, thanks," to the selfie-stick sellers. They're usually immigrants to Britain, just trying to make a pound.

Every big UK[32] or European city has phone thieves and pickpockets, but even the great Rick Steves has only been pickpocketed once and not in London. I've been all over Italy and to London, and I've never seen a pickpocket or been worried about one. Just upload your phone photos every night, keep your passport in your hotel (some guidebooks say to carry a photocopy, but I don't even do that), and don't stash tons of cash in your pocket.

---

for using shoddy business practices.

[31] Jaywalking is crossing a street outside the crosswalk. In tourist areas, London crosswalks have big messages painted on the pavement: "look right" or "look left."

[32] "UK" is short for United Kingdom of Great Britain and Northern Ireland. Great Britain is England, Wales, and Scotland. The south of Ireland is a republic.

Pickpockets, who are often children, pick pockets when their targets are distracted by an accomplice, a street performer, or a street artisan, so be a little more careful in those situations. If you are carrying a backpack in a crowd of people, shift it to your front (and don't carry cash in it). My dad had his backpack unzipped and money stolen while it was on his back in Lisbon, Portugal, in 1982. So it happens.

Over the past few years, London has suffered a few terrorist attacks (as have cities in Europe and the United States). These attacks are very rare. I'm guessing that you are more likely to get hit by a car in London than to get blown up in a London terror attack. That's how rare these attacks really are. So don't worry about them.

Food

Breakfast

You'll probably have this at the hotel's breakfast buffet. Brits like baked beans for breakfast and not good ones either, so there may be some of those at the buffet. Try them and be done with it. Their cereals are pretty much the same as ours but with different names.

Lunch

For lunch, I'm going to tell you something different from every other travel book. In London, buy some food at an American fast-food chain, like McDonald's. Everyone will think you are crazy to travel so far to eat American food, but it's not American food.

The menus of American fast-food restaurants overseas are a little different than in the United States. In Australia, McDonald's fries can come with truffle mayo. In Rome,

Burger King serves tiramisu for dessert. So in London, try something different, like a McDonald's Cadbury Dairy Milk McFlurry or a chocolate-filled donut, called a "chocolatey" donut.

When you do it, be sure to take a selfie with the restaurant's logo (e.g., golden arches) and the non-American food item to show your friends back home. Also, don't be surprised if you have to order and pay for your food at a video-screen kiosk and then pick up the food at the counter.

Otherwise, if you are walking around and getting hungry, there are two places to get sandwiches: Pret a Manger and Little Waitrose. They are all over London. Pret a Mangers are a cross between Subway and Starbucks, and a lot of them are nice inside and are good places to sit down (or take the food to go). They'll make you a sandwich and a latte, which you pay for when you place your order. Bus your own table.

Little Waitroses don't have tables; you buy your food and eat it in a park or while you walk. Little Waitroses are small, upscale grocery stores selling a large selection of fresh food and awesome premade sandwiches to take out. Some sandwiches are a little different, like the egg mayo with charred asparagus, but they sell simpler sandwiches too, and they tack on an extra 5p for each plastic grocery bag. That little tax has cut plastic bag use in London by 85 percent. That's six billion bags out of circulation. So buy one bag, and reuse it for the rest of your stay in London.

Dinner

Many books and websites discuss London restaurants. I'm assuming that you are going to have dinner with your family. For dining ideas, do your homework ahead of time by looking in some of the famous guide books. I can recommend

Chinatown's Wong Kei restaurant, not so much for the food but because the waiters are intentionally rude. One of them didn't think I ordered enough food and told me so, and another filled our water glasses from the water beaker on the table next to us. Be sure to talk back to them. My cousin made the waiters refill her water glass ten times. I also liked Jamie Oliver's Diner (he has three different restaurants in London) where you can get some American-tasting food or British food. You'll probably need a reservation there.

Buying Stuff

Britain is not a haggling country, so the price is generally the price, even in a market like Covent Gardens. Keep your receipts just in case you need to show them to the US customs officer to verify the prices of things you are bringing back into the United States.

Places to See and Things to Do

I'm not saying you have to ditch your parents, but there are probably some things they want to do that you don't want to do and vice versa, so why not split up for a while? I've made two lists. You might find things on either list that ought to be switched. That's cool—use my lists as a starter, reorganize them, and make them your own.

Also, there are a million things to do and see in London. No list is complete. The next time I go, I'm going to try some of the famous old swimming pools there.

Without Your Parents

The London Eye is a giant Ferris wheel, which is often featured in movies set in London. It's located right on the river Thames. The ticket seller at the base wouldn't let me on because I was fifteen years old then and with my cousin, who was sixteen. Sixteen-year-olds can ride, but fifteen-year-olds need a guardian who is eighteen or older.

Even so, the area around the base of the Eye is open to all and has a festive atmosphere. It's a fun place to be and to look at people.

Covent Gardens has been an open-air market for four centuries or more with lots of small stalls. I could wander around there looking at its curiosities for several hours.

Piccadilly Circus is a shopping district with lots of clothing stores. The stores aren't cheap, but there are a lot of them up and down rows of streets. It's more like Fifth Avenue, NY, than Covent Gardens.

Platform 9¾ at King's Cross Station has a shopping cart stuck partly in a wall and a Harry Potter gift store next door. It's in the lobby, not on the real train platforms where you need a train ticket to get in. Get there early or late, or the lines will be long to stand holding the cart and posing like Harry Potter on his way to Hogwarts.

The Changing of the Guard at Buckingham Palace has immense crowds. It's the very formal ceremony where the palace guards switch out for fresh guards. If you want to see the whole thing, you'll have to go early and go two or three times, standing in different places, to see all parts of it. If you're going once, get to the Palace at least forty minutes early, and stand right up against the fence. You'll be crushed into the fence. The cops will yell at you if you climb on the fence to see better.

The big monument with steps in front of Buckingham Palace[33] is the Victoria Memorial. That's a good place to see the guard march by but not so good to see the stuff going on inside the fence.

Every little thing about the changing of the guards has symbolism in it, from the flags they carry to the pace of their marches to the songs the band plays. If that interests you, Google "changing of the guards," and find a link that explains everything. No country does pageantry better than the British, and the Changing of the Guard is one of their best displays. I can't imagine something like that in America. On the whole, the flash of it isn't worth it to us, I suppose.

Trafalgar Square street performers and artists are fun to watch and to buy stuff from. The square is big with fountains, art, and busts of military heroes—and lots of

---

[33] The original house here was owned by John Sheffield, Duke of Buckingham, and that's how the palace got its name.

tourists. I'm not sure lots of tourists come to London to hang out at the square itself, but they should. The tourists are there because the square is bordered by the National Gallery, St Martin-in-the-Fields Church, the Mall (a road often closed to traffic) leading to Buckingham Palace, Admiralty Arch, and two other major roads—Whitehall and the Strand.[34]

Most tourists see the square on their way to somewhere else. But while your parents are dragging their way through the National Gallery, go hang out there, and take a selfie with one of the giant metal lions at the base of Nelson's Column. You can't miss them.

St. James Park is a green space with ponds and gardens between the Horse Guards building and parade ground and Buckingham Palace. In nice weather it's a nice place to hang out, and it's near an Underground station and 10 Downing Street.

The Horse Guards building is at the other end of St. James Park from Buckingham Palace. It has a large parade ground on the St. James Park side and a passage to walk through to Whitehall Street. You can get really close to the guards in their horse-tailed helmets, and you can pet their horses, which are usually Irish Warmbloods. The changing of the horse guards is a small ceremony and is not crowded by tourists.

---

[34] London has five kinds of pedestrian crossings, nicknamed Zebra, Pelican, Puffin, Toucan, and Pegasus, as well as pedestrian "sanctuaries," which are islands to stand on in the middle of the street. Pegasus crossings are for horse riders as well as for pedestrians and have an additional crossing signal button high up for riders to press. You'll see wiggly lines, like french fries laid out end-to-end, painted on the street before the crossings. These are meant to warn drivers that a crosswalk is coming up. London is a relatively safe place for pedestrians as long as you remember to look right, then left, then right before crossing.

The National Gallery holds many important paintings. If you don't like paintings, then the place is boring. You'll get much more out of it by taking some kind of descriptive tour of the gallery because the tours will point out details that you'll miss on your own and will put the paintings in context with each other. Rick Steves's London guidebook has a nice tour (but our edition of the book was a bit old, and the gallery had moved some paintings), and the gallery rents audio guides. The gallery has a lot of rooms, and it's easy to get lost or separated from the rest of your group. The rooms are numbered, which helps.

If you like the National Gallery, Google "galleries in London" for a list of other galleries to visit. Some charge admission; the National Gallery takes donations.

The MI6 building is right next to the Vauxhall Bridge, and the view of it is good from the bridge. It's James Bond's headquarters, and it was blown up by computer magic in the movie *Skyfall*, the twenty-third James Bond movie. It's a twenty-minute walk south of Big Ben and is probably not worth it unless you really like James Bond.

Ye Olde Cheshire Cheese is a pub built in 1666 after London's great fire. Charles Dickens is said to have written *A Tale of Two Cities* in the pub. I'm not sure the food is great there, but since you have to eat in at least one pub in London, just to say you did, you might as well eat there.

10 Downing Street is the prime minister's residence—basically the White House of the United Kingdom. It's not much to look at from the outside, but it's worth a selfie since you'll probably be walking right by it after passing Big Ben.

Royal Albert Hall is a beautiful concert hall and is worth a look. It's even better if you see a show there. Google "Royal Albert Hall" to see pictures of it and a schedule of shows, from Cirque du Soleil to classical music to popular music.

The Shard, the Gherkin, and the City Hall are all cool modern buildings that are tall and twisted. Everyone comes to London to see the old stuff, but these buildings are worth seeing. Google them to find out where they are.

Hyde Park is more or less another green space. It's the largest of the four royal parks. It was originally owned by Westminster Abbey, but Henry VIII took it for a hunting ground in 1536. England is full of places like that—simple places that have interesting histories. There were 172 recorded duels there in the eighteenth century. It has the first lighted road in London, which was lighted to deter robbers.

Big Ben and Parliament are also great choices. You have to take a selfie with Big Ben—London's famous clock tower. It's right at the end of the Houses of Parliament, which is the home of the British government.

Kayaking or canoeing London is a great way to see the place from a view most people don't get to see. You'll want to take a guided trip so that someone can explain everything you see.

You can see a zoo back home, so there isn't really a reason to go to the London Zoo. I put it on the list because it's a good place for your smaller siblings to blow off steam.

Lee Valley White Water Centre was part of the 2012 London Olympics. You can probably find a warmer place than London to whitewater raft back at home, but this is something not many tourists will do.

The House of Dreams is a house in East Dulwich covered with trash art. It's pretty cool but is too far to walk from, say, Parliament.

The Vertical Chill in London is an indoor ice-climbing venue. If I have to explain it, you don't want to do it. (vertical-chill.com)

With Your Parents

High tea is tea, fancy sandwiches, and pastries served in a comfortable setting. This is one of the coolest things to do in London, although you can do it in the United States too. Lots of places serve high tea, but for a good atmosphere, you'll want one that's been doing it for a long time. We had a fine time at Brown's Hotel, which has been a hotel since 1837. Be sure and get high tea reservations before you leave home.

The Tower Bridge, not to be confused with the London Bridge, is great to visit because you can climb to the top and walk over a clear floor. Plus, from the top, the views of London are exceptional. There is a fee to tour the bridge, and the price of the tour includes touring the engine room of the bridge, which uses hydraulics to raise and lower the middle part. Unless you like engines, you can skip that part.

The Tower of London is an old prison and fort that now holds England's crown jewels and a historical museum with Henry VIII's armor, old weapons, and other similar items. It's more interesting than I'm making it sound. The jewels (crowns and other royal artifacts with gems and such) are cool and are not something you'll see anywhere else in the world.

The Tower has free guided tours with uniformed "Beefeaters," (their full title is the Yeomen Warders of Her Majesty's Royal

Palace and Fortress the Tower of London, and Members of the Sovereign's Body Guard of the Yeoman Guard Extraordinary) which are ceremonial guards who are long-serving, retired military noncommissioned officers. The Beefeaters' tours are often dramatic and full of bloody stories—botched executions and murdered royal children—reflecting the bloody history of the Tower.

The Tower also has a flock of ravens that live there under the care of a Beefeater called the Ravenmaster, so you'll see ravens walking around. They have a clipped wing, which keeps them on the Tower grounds, but they still fly. Ravens have been there for centuries.

But in my opinion, the coolest thing to see is the ancient graffiti scratched into the walls by prisoners, many of whom were awaiting execution.

The British National Archives is where old documents are kept. It has everything from an original Beatles song lyric sheet to a Bach manuscript to a Gutenberg Bible to a hundreds-year-old swimming manual. My dad loves this place, but to me, once you've seen twenty illuminated[35] books, you've seen them all.

London's West End is its theater district with musicals and plays like Broadway in New York. Go see a show there some evening. We watched *The Mousetrap*, which is the West End's longest running play. It's a family-friendly mystery written by Agatha Christie. We got lost several times on the way to the St. Martin's Theater, so leave a little early.

The British Museum has the Rosetta Stone and about eight million other cultural art objects and antiquities. The area

---

[35] "Illuminated" is the word for the decorative art in the margins of ancient books.

around the Rosetta Stone can get crowded. It's hard to go to London and not go to the British Museum; it's the best of its kind in the world. That said, if you're not really interested in ancient Assyrian statues and the like, then it's kind of a waste of time but not a waste of money. It's free. If you go, do some kind of guided tour—either self-guided with a book or with a rented audio tour or with a tour guide.

Westminster Abbey is a working church, and the spot it is on has had a church on it for one thousand years. You can attend a service or organ recital there or just listen to the hourly prayer inside. My cousin fell asleep during an organ recital there, but it was our first day, and we were jet-lagged pretty badly. The Abbey is a lot more than a church. It's the place where kings and queens are coronated and where royal weddings take place. Everyone who is anyone in Britain is buried or memorialized there. The floors and walls are covered with names and tombs, from the Tomb of the Unknown Warrior to John Andre, the British Officer hanged by George Washington for conspiring with Benedict Arnold. Poet's Corner holds the tombs and memorials of writers, including Chaucer.

It isn't free to enter, but the fee comes with an audio-tour headset.

The Globe Theater is a reproduction of the theater that Shakespeare partly owned and performed in. It's easy to get to by river bus by using your Oyster card.

Running and Swimming

My stepmother would ask, "Why would you fly all the way to London just to do something that you could do at home for free?" She has a point, but a run is a great way to get a feel for a place, and London has some great jogging paths (Google "jogging in London") through different kinds of places, including towpaths. The paths might not be near your hotel, but the Underground should get you there. It might even be worth an Uber.

I didn't swim in London, but if you are a swimmer and feel the need for a swim, singer and songwriter Loudon Wainright III suggests some famous ponds: the Kenwood Ladies' Bathing Pond and the Highgate Men's Bathing Pond. There are a lot of old, classic pools and ponds to swim in, in London. Note that the Brits call an outdoor pool a "lido," as in the Parliament Hill Lido.

Coming Home

The Airport

Coming home is pretty much like going to London. First, you go through security, and then there is a lot of waiting and looking for places to charge your phone. One thing that is different is the duty-free shop. These are stores in the airport past security that sell all kinds of things but without the British taxes on them. So, in theory, they should be less expensive because things aren't taxed, but that's not always the case, so be careful about the prices. Anyway, it's always free to look—and touch.

The Flight Home

The flight home should be pretty much like the flight there, except the food may be a bit different. Planes load up on food at the airport they are leaving from, so when you leave, you'll be getting English food for the trip home.

The cool thing is that you'll leave in the morning, and because you're flying west, you will be back home in the United States by the afternoon—no painful overnight flight.

As you approach the United States, the flight attendants will pass around blue customs declaration forms[36] to each family (blood relations, like cousins, are family). If you are traveling with someone as a nonfamily member (e.g., your boyfriend's family), you will need to fill out your own form. Otherwise, some responsible adult in your group will fill this out for everyone. That person will write the value, in dollars, of all of the things you bought. If the total is over $800, someone in

[36] If you want to see one, Google "US customs declaration form," and click on www.cbp.gov.

your family might have to pay duty (a tax) on the amount over $800.

My family has never been close to $800, but we're cheap. I'm not going to tell you how to break the law, but if the tags fall off the clothes you bought in London, it may be hard for the customs officer to tell where they come from, unless the t-shirt says something like, "mind the gap" or "I went to London and all I got was this shirt."

US customs officers have never looked too closely at me or my family. I wouldn't worry about it, unless you are trying to smuggle in some expensive objects, like silver or jewelry.

Dublin, Ireland

If you leave London for the United States via Dublin, you'll pass through US customs and passport control in Dublin, rather than the usual way on US soil at whatever international airport you land at.

Here is the trick. Grab the hotel room pen as you leave for the airport; you'll need it there. As you wind your way through Dublin International Airport, hauling all your bags, give your parents a heads-up to pick up a blue US customs form at the first opportunity. Pens and blue forms run out. When they take the form, give them the pen you took from the hotel room. Now you're a hero.

The customs declaration form seems more like a formality in Dublin because customs there uses some modern electronic kiosks that ask blue-form questions again, scan your passport picture, take a picture of your face, and then print it all out. Don't worry if the machine can't match the passport photo to the new picture. If that happens, the machine printout of your face will come out with an X on it. I think that just tells the border officer to take a closer look. My dad always gets the X, but he gets through just fine.

Customs and Passport Control Back Home

After the plane lands, you'll head to customs and passport control with the blue customs declaration form.

Jet Lag Again

Jet lag going from east to west (London to the United States) is much easier to get over. You should be all right in several days.

What to Tell Your Friends When You Get Home

Some of the chocolate[37] in the United Kingdom is different from what we have in the United States, so bring some back for your friends. It's not fancy chocolate from an expensive store; it's just the chocolate from Little Waitrose or another grocery or drugstore.[38]

Of course, you'll show your friends photo places you visited and toured while in London and the United Kingdom, including, I'm sure, the airports and your hotel. That's actually a good idea. People at home are more interested in the small differences between societies than in seeing a picture of a church that they could Google if they wanted to.

So take pictures of your hotel's bathroom and toilet and of the beans at the breakfast buffet. Sure, the other guests will think you're weird, but so what? Take pictures of road signs, car license plates, hotel elevator buttons (what we call the first floor the Brits call zero), the way grapes are sold in boxes, and anything else that is a little different from home.

There is a lot of stuff about London that's not on the Internet. Show them what it is. And mind the gap.

---

[37] If you are visiting friends in the United Kingdom, bring them different varieties of M&Ms. They don't have all the different kinds we have here.
[38] Drugstores are called *chemists* in Britain.

Other Books by Richard Evans

Fiction
Animal Earrings

Nonfiction Statistics Books

The Pocket Reference for Veterinary Statistical Analyses
Bayesian Inference When the Pooling of Data Is Uncertain
Happy Stats: Guidelines for Harmonious Statistical Collaborations

Find his new books at **amazon.com/author/richevans**.

Made in the USA
Middletown, DE
08 December 2023

45042768R00031